Tap Tap!

by Joanna Lake

illustrated by Genie Espinosa

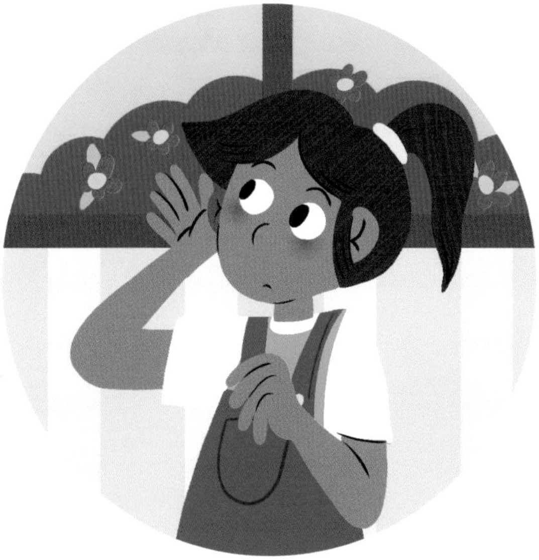

OXFORD
UNIVERSITY PRESS

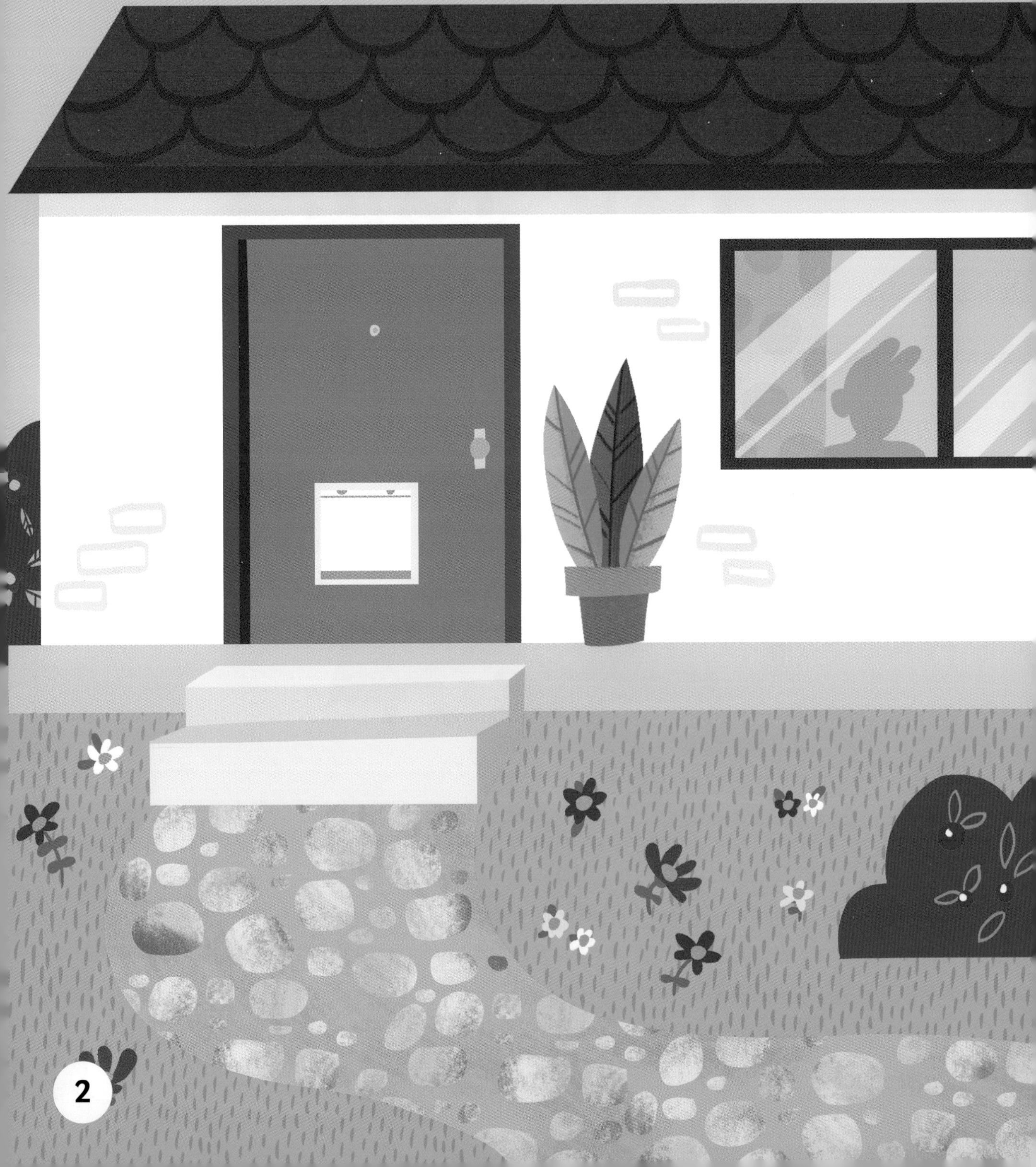

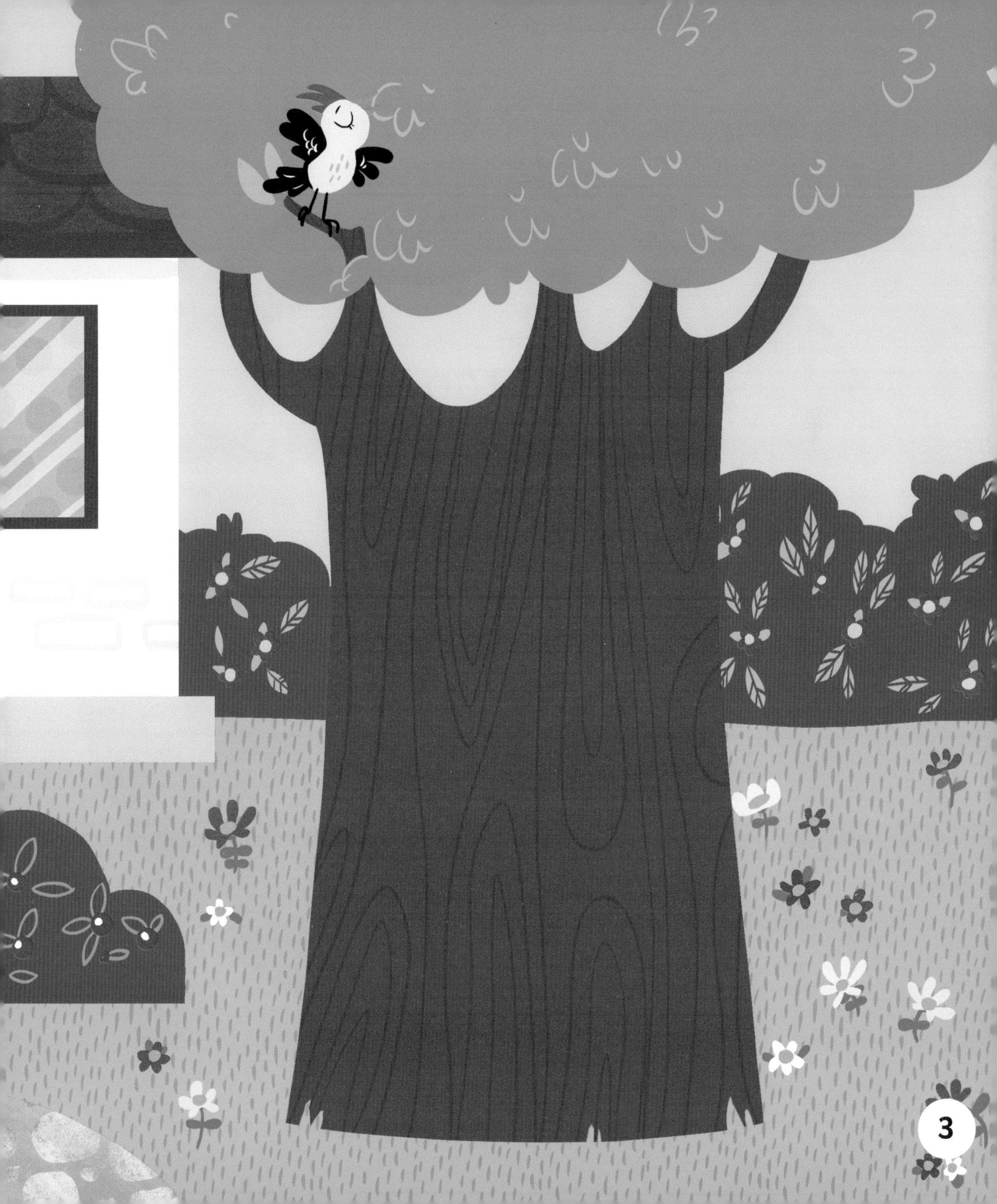

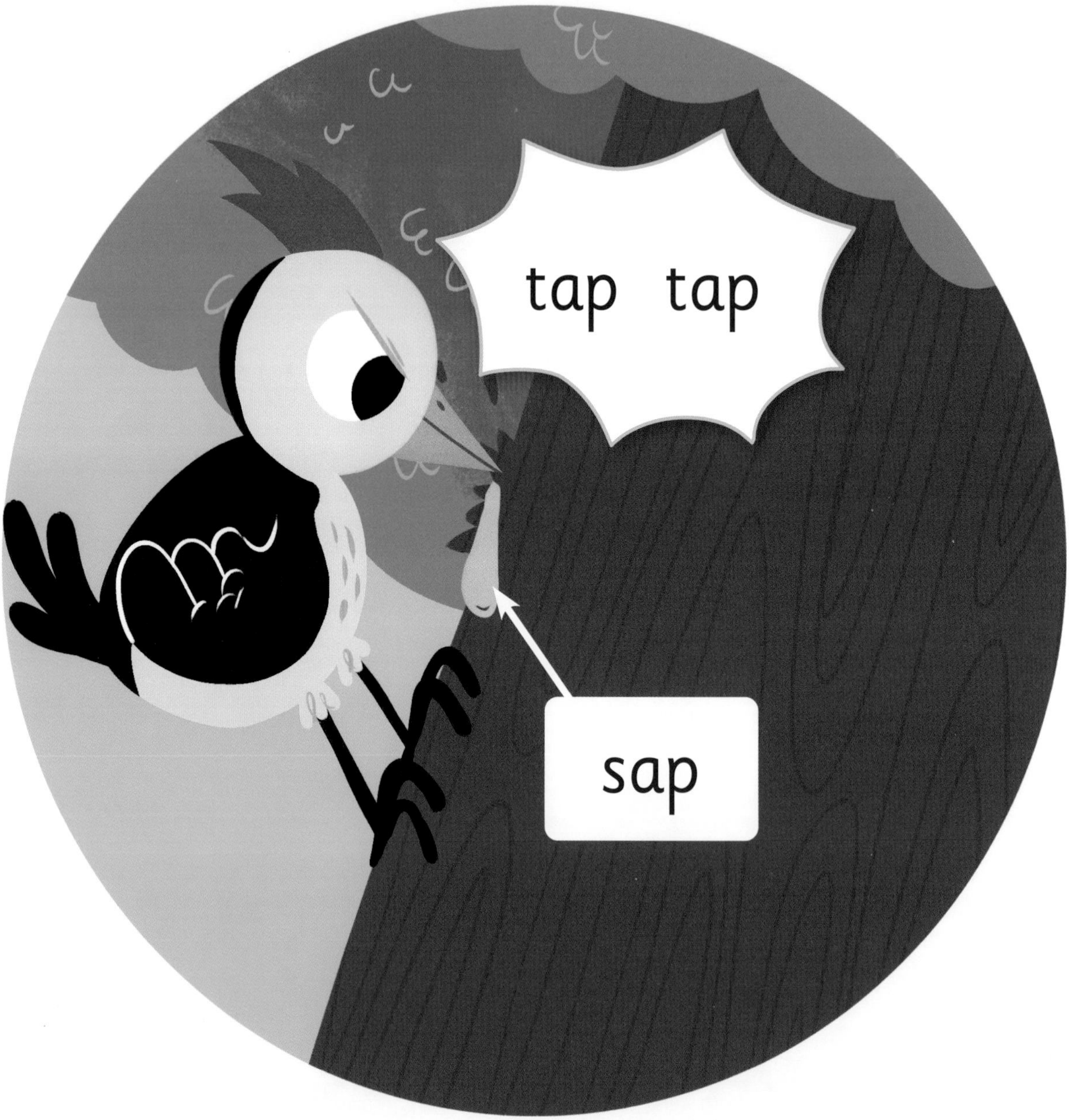
tap tap
sap

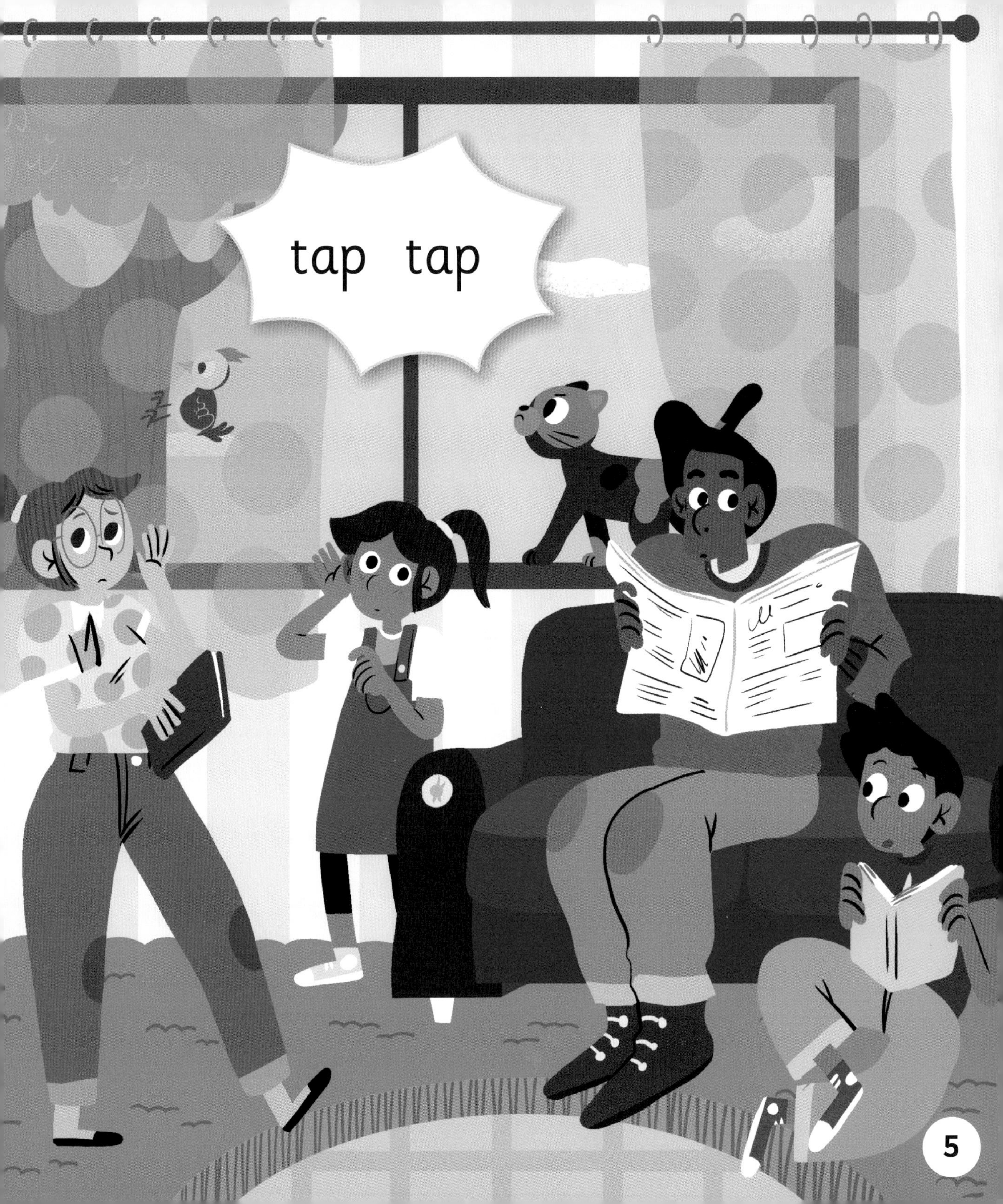
tap tap

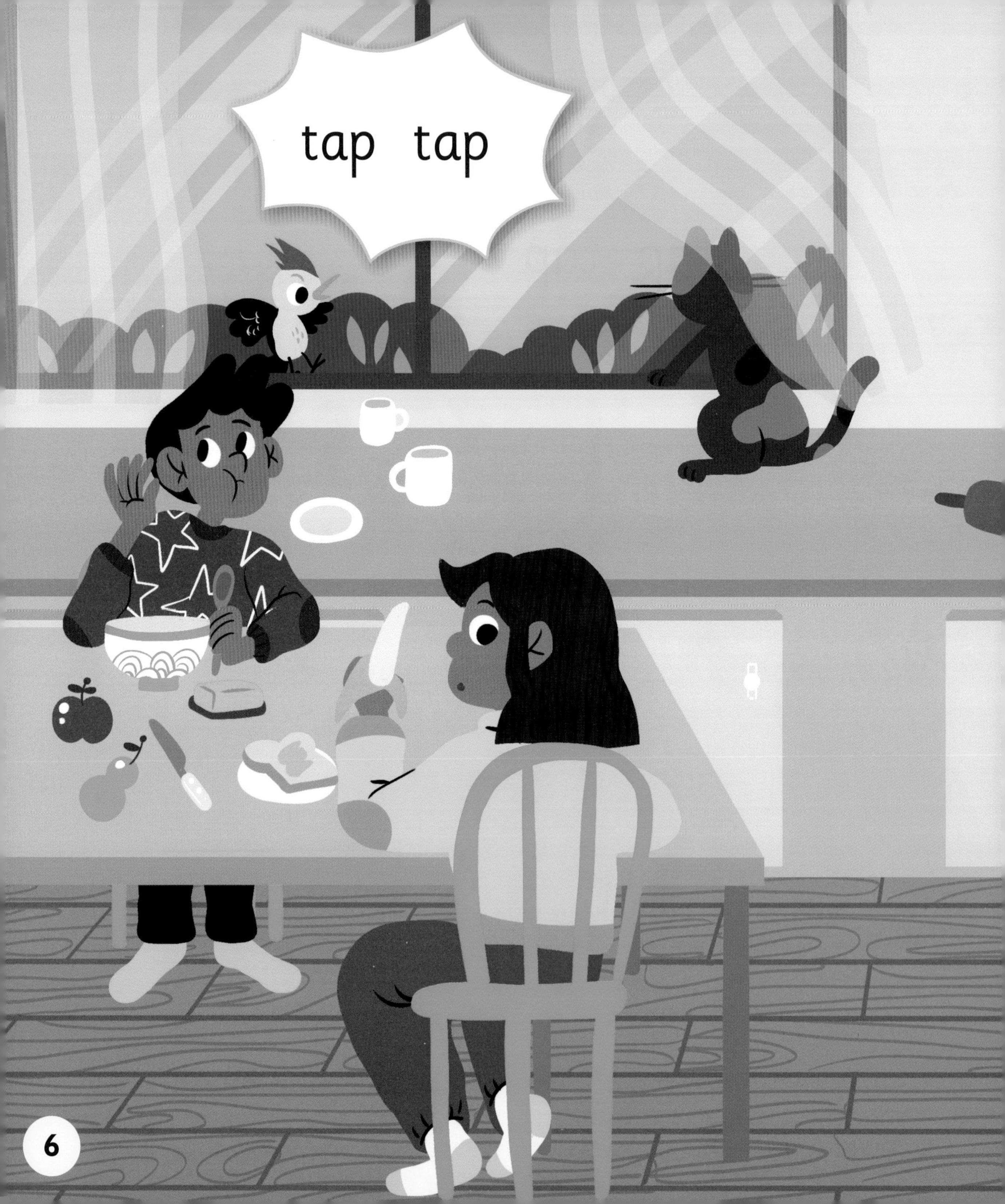
tap tap

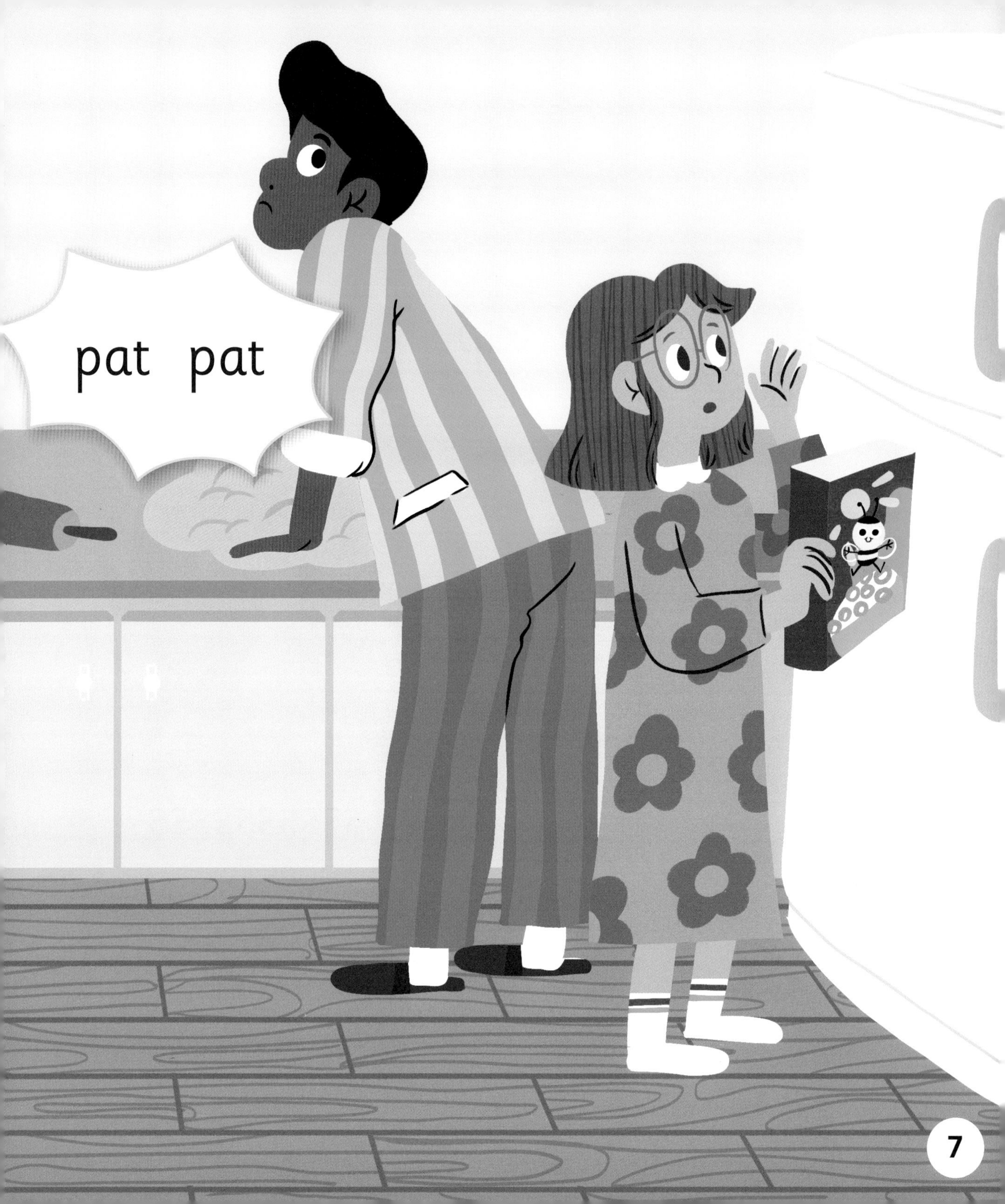
pat pat

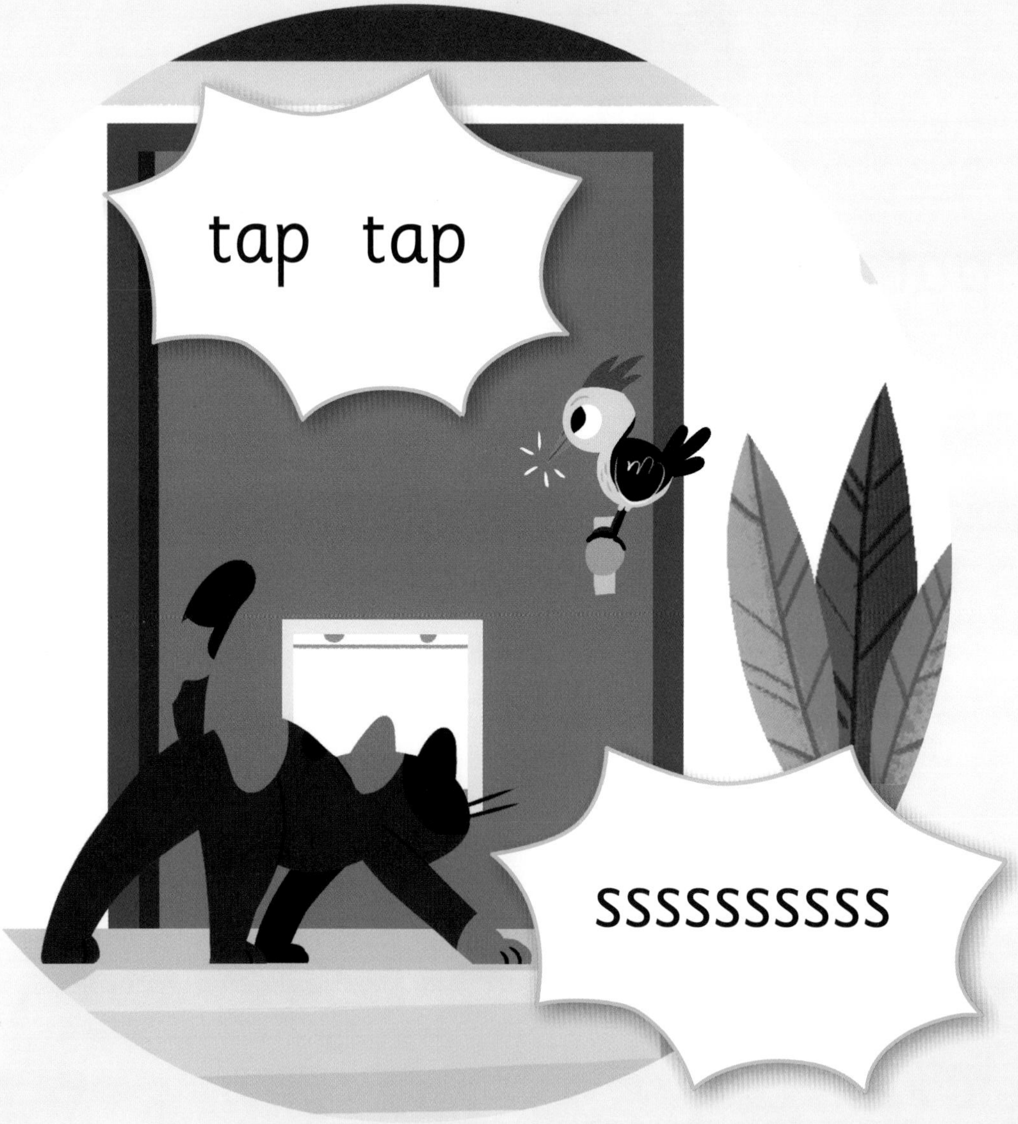
tap tap
sssssssss

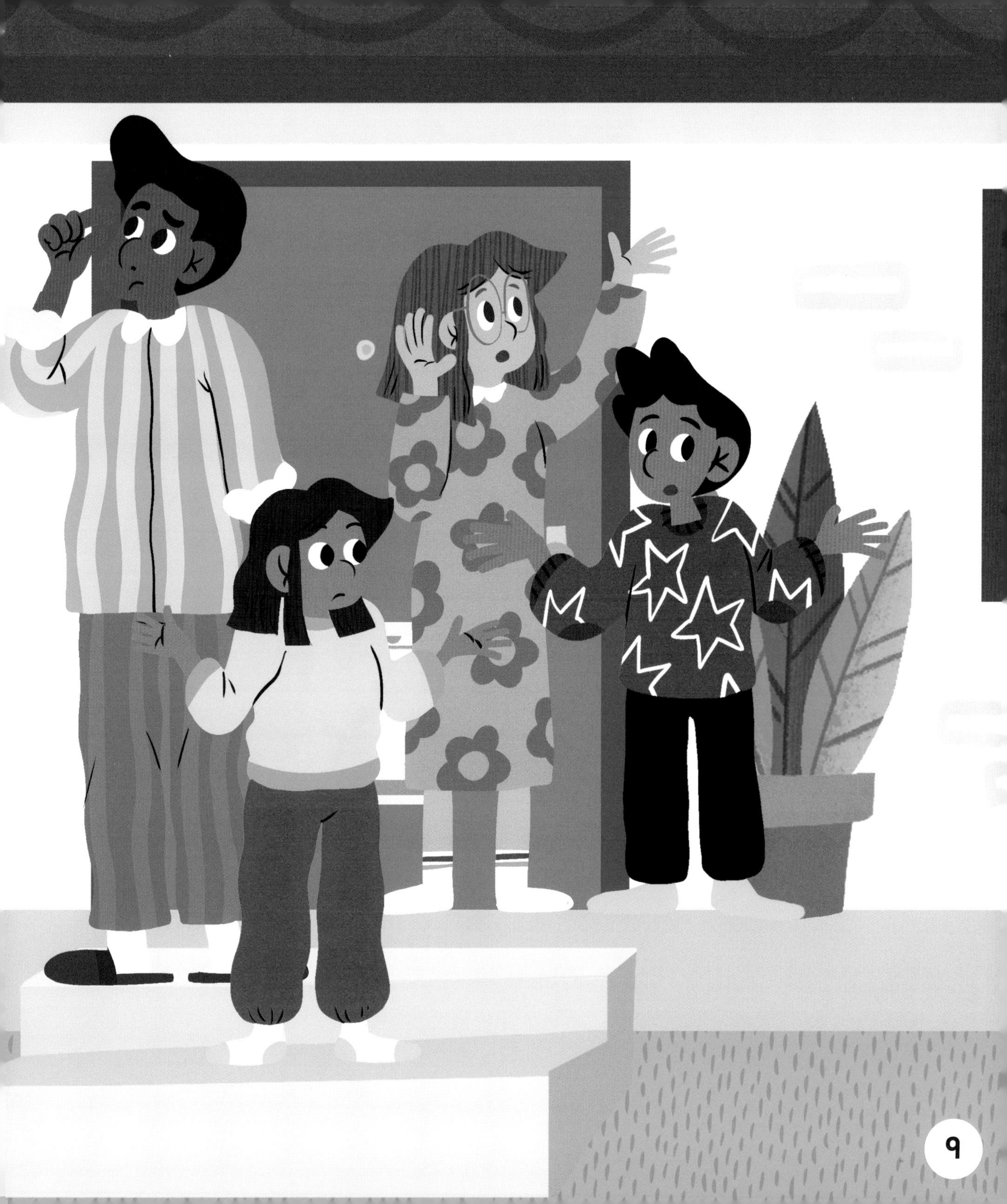

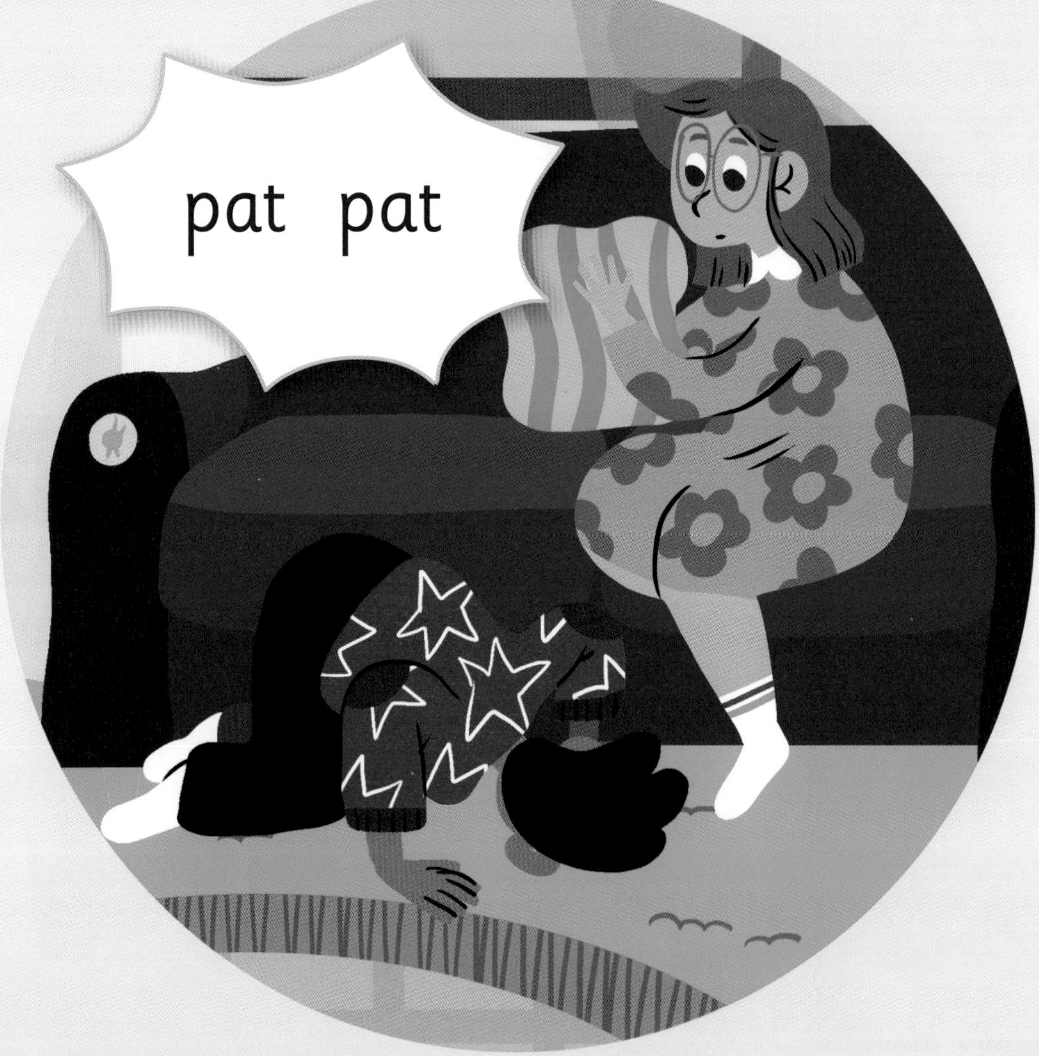
pat pat

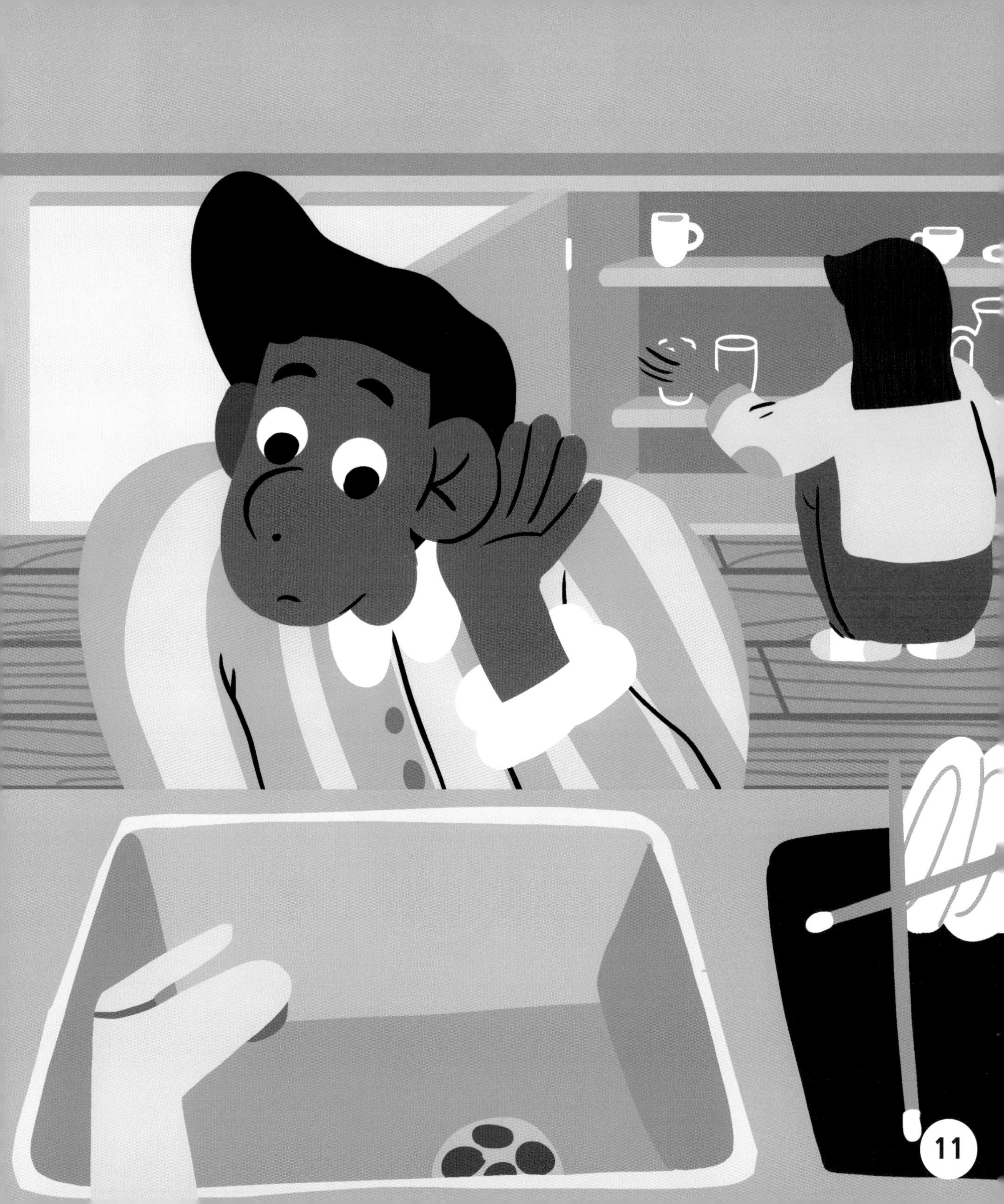

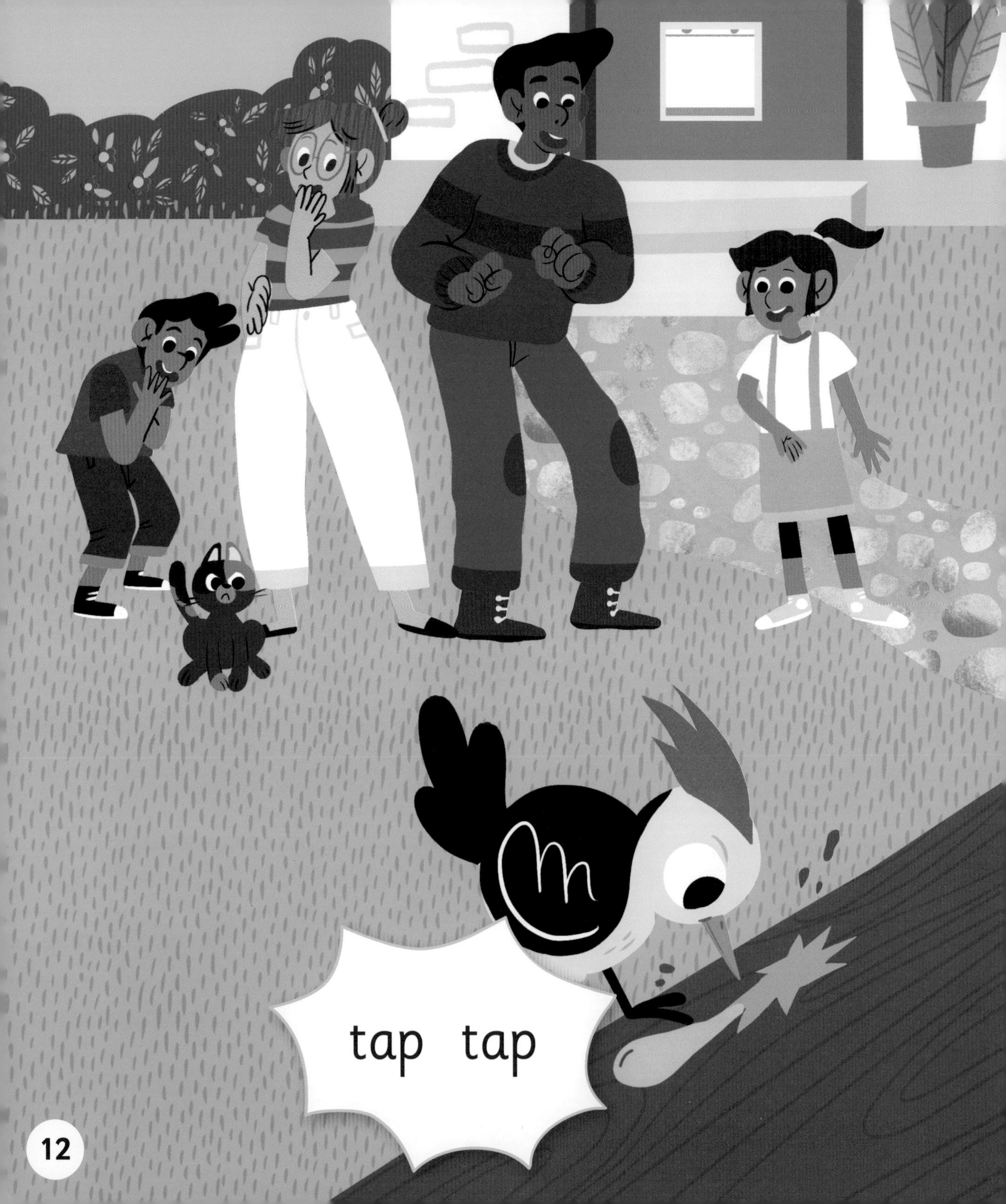
tap tap